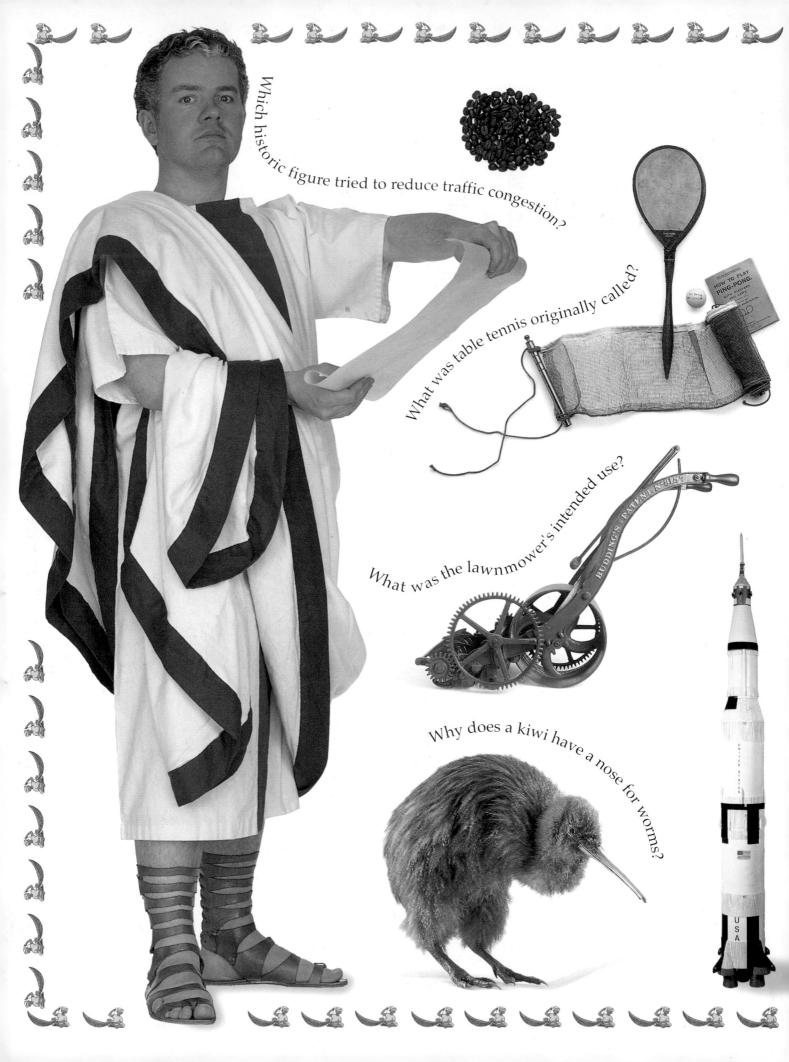

Which historic figure tried to reduce traffic congestion?

What was table tennis originally called?

What was the lawnmower's intended use?

Why does a kiwi have a nose for worms?

# AMAZING FACTS

Why are male seahorses such devoted fathers?

How was acupuncture discovered?

Written by
## Ned Halley

## DORLING KINDERSLEY
London • New York • Stuttgart • Moscow • Sydney

# DK

## A DORLING KINDERSLEY BOOK
www.dk.com

Which plant will render you speechless?

Why are male moths so sensitive?

**Editor** Marie Twist
**Art editor** Iain Morris
**Managing editor** Linda Martin
**Senior managing art editor** Julia Harris
**DTP designer** Nicky Studdart
**Production** Lisa Moss
**Picture research** Melissa Albany

First published in Great Britain in 1997
by Dorling Kindersley Limited,
9 Henrietta Street, London WC2E 8PS

A CIP catalogue record for this book is
available from the British Library.

ISBN 0 7513 5517 8

Colour reproduction by Colourscan, Singapore
Printed in Italy by LEGO.

How did a baby fly?

Why are bloodhounds such reliable detectives?

# Contents

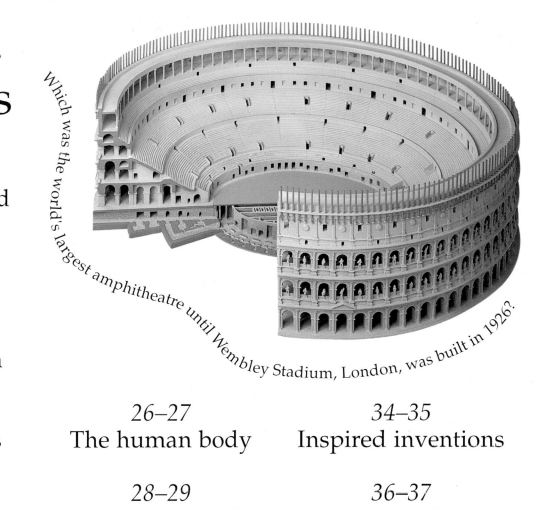

Which was the world's largest amphitheatre until Wembley Stadium, London, was built in 1926?

Which is the most translated book in the world?

# Out of this world

SPACE STRETCHES the imagination to the limit – and beyond. Our star, the Sun, at the centre of a solar system 12 billion kilometres wide, is one of 100 billion stars in our galaxy. Countless other galaxies lie further out in the Universe – but even the nearest, Andromeda, is so distant that it takes light, travelling at 300,000 km (186,000 miles) per second, two million years to reach it. Today, these places and their secrets seem impossibly out of reach. But with space travel now a reality, amazing discoveries are surely just a matter of time.

**By Jove**
Jupiter is 1,300 times the size of Earth, and its years are 12 times longer.

*An astronaut orbiting Earth sees the sun rise and set 15 times a day*

**Very heavy**
The Sun makes up over 99 per cent of our solar system's weight.

**Very bright**
In one second, the Sun produces 35 million times the average yearly electricity supply used in the whole of North America.

**Drink problem**
In space, astronauts use straws or squirt drinks into their mouths with a dispenser like a water pistol. Liquid in a cup would form into a free-floating ball-like mass.

**Keeping cool**
Apollo spacecraft fuel tanks were so well insulated that if you filled one with ice, it would take more than eight years to melt.

*Food for future manned space flights may be grown on board the spacecraft*

**Dog dazed**
Meteorites commonly hit Earth, but the only living creature known to have been killed by one was a dog, struck at Nakhla, Egypt, in 1911.

**Incredible journey**
Cosmonaut Valery Ryuminhas travelled the equivalent of 5,750 round-the-world trips – further than the distance from Earth to Mars and back.

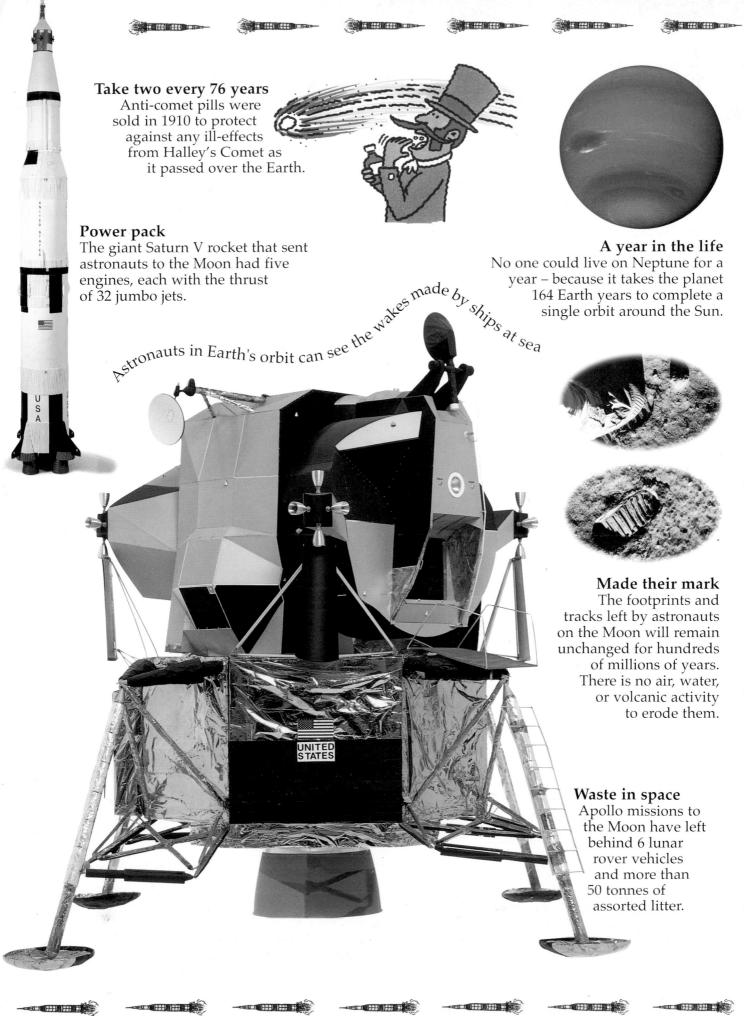

### Take two every 76 years
Anti-comet pills were sold in 1910 to protect against any ill-effects from Halley's Comet as it passed over the Earth.

### Power pack
The giant Saturn V rocket that sent astronauts to the Moon had five engines, each with the thrust of 32 jumbo jets.

Astronauts in Earth's orbit can see the wakes made by ships at sea

### A year in the life
No one could live on Neptune for a year – because it takes the planet 164 Earth years to complete a single orbit around the Sun.

### Made their mark
The footprints and tracks left by astronauts on the Moon will remain unchanged for hundreds of millions of years. There is no air, water, or volcanic activity to erode them.

### Waste in space
Apollo missions to the Moon have left behind 6 lunar rover vehicles and more than 50 tonnes of assorted litter.

# Planet Earth

ROCKS TURN INTO GIANT MUSHROOM SHAPES, crops are flattened into strange, unearthly patterns, showers of living creatures fall as rain from the sky. All are the work of that most unpredictable of life forces – the weather. Largely produced by the evaporation of the great oceans and seas that cover three-quarters of the Earth, rain (and the accompanying storms and deluges), together with wind, shape not only our lives, but the very surface of our world.

Journeying east-west in the former USSR covered seven time zones

**They came from the sky**
Trowbridge in England once had an unusual downpour – of frogs. Strong winds had sucked them up from local ponds and rivers.

**Quick thaw**
In South Dakota, USA, the temperature once rose from a freezing -20° C (4° F) to a mild 7° C (45° F) – in two minutes.

**Never strikes twice?**
An American park ranger was hit by lightning seven times in 25 years. He lost his hair and eyebrows, but survived.

Lightning can reach a speed of 140,000 kms (87,000 mps)

**Whirlwind action**
A tornado in Minnesota, USA, lifted an 83-tonne train 25 m (80 ft) into the air and dropped it in a ditch.

### Sea shanty
A beach on the Scottish island of Eigg sings! Sand sifted through the fingers emits musical tones.

### Absolutely brilliant
A postage-stamp-size section of the Sun's surface produces more light than 500 60-watt bulbs. That's enough to light 48 homes.

### Added salt
If all the salt in the oceans and seas was collected up, it would cover the whole of the Earth's land surface in a layer 152 m (500 ft) thick.

### It never stops
The Earth travels through space at more than 106,200 km/h (66,000 mph) and, at the equator, is spinning round at 1,700 km/h (1,000 mph).

### Halfcocked
Hurricanes spin anti-clockwise north of the equator, and clockwise south of the equator.

### Uplifting experience
In Ancona, Italy, a tornado picked up a pram, complete with sleeping baby, and set it down safely 100 m (400 ft) away.

### Getting through
If an excavator could dig a tunnel through the Earth at a rate of 1 m (3 ft) per hour, it would take 1,440 years to reach the other side.

The Pacific ocean fills nearly half the globe

# Inside the Earth

MOST OF US KNOW diamonds are forever, because they are so hard. But did you realize they are 90 times harder than any other natural material found on Earth? Another miraculous mineral among the world's riches is gold – which is so indestructible that more than half the quantity ever found in history is still in circulation. These natural marvels are created over millions of years by the tremendous changes that take place in the Earth's crust, and the violent events, such as earthquakes and volcanic eruptions that accompany them.

### Lava bread
Bread was preserved intact after a volcanic eruption in Pompeii, Italy. Ash had turned loaves to carbon.

### Hot rock
Diamond is the hardest natural substance on Earth. Able to withstand extreme heat, it enabled an infrared radiometer on the Pioneer space probe to operate at temperatures of 450° C (840° F) near the surface of the planet Venus.

### Navigator
The secret of how birds migrate over great distances is thought to lie in a tiny crystal in their brains that detects the Earth's magnetic field.

### Soft to the touch
The rare metal Gallium will melt in the heat of your hand if held for a short time.

*Every year there are over a million earthquakes, mostly tiny tremors too small to be felt*

### Making waves
The first seismoscope – for detecting earthquakes – was invented by Chinese geographer Chang Heng in AD 132.

### Bubble bath
Swimming in lakes near volcanoes is very risky. Volcanic gases can dissolve in the water, making it so acidic it can burn through human flesh.

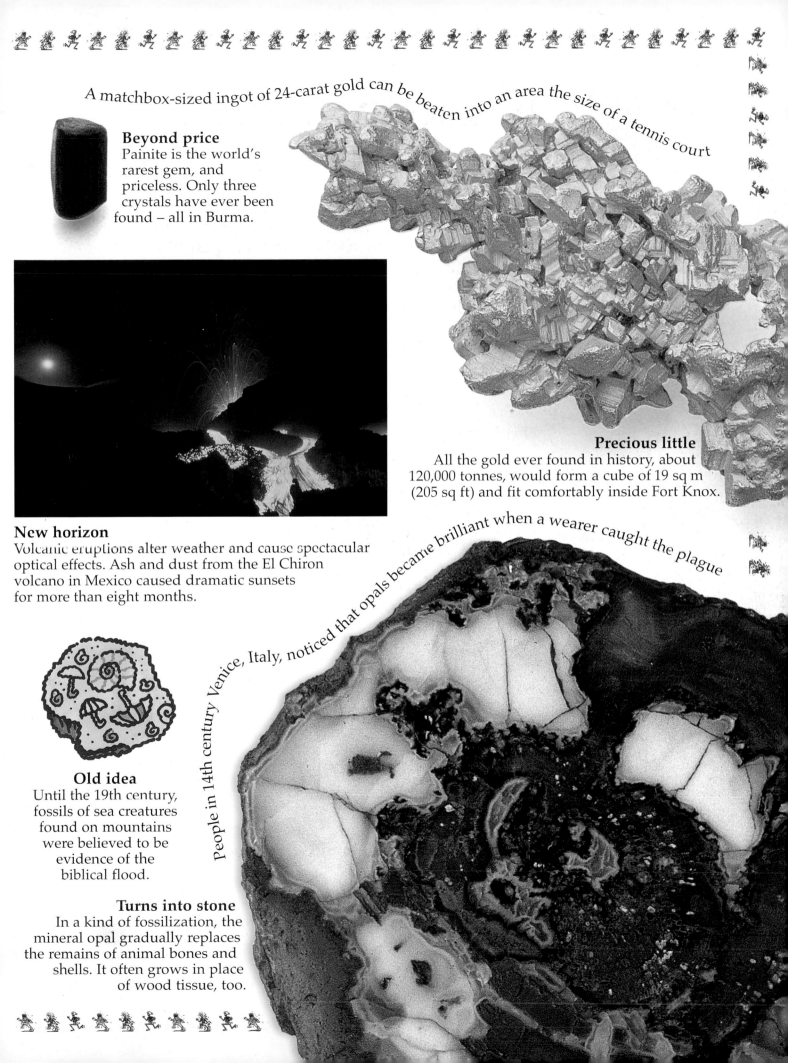

A matchbox-sized ingot of 24-carat gold can be beaten into an area the size of a tennis court

### Beyond price
Painite is the world's rarest gem, and priceless. Only three crystals have ever been found – all in Burma.

### Precious little
All the gold ever found in history, about 120,000 tonnes, would form a cube of 19 sq m (205 sq ft) and fit comfortably inside Fort Knox.

### New horizon
Volcanic eruptions alter weather and cause spectacular optical effects. Ash and dust from the El Chiron volcano in Mexico caused dramatic sunsets for more than eight months.

People in 14th century Venice, Italy, noticed that opals became brilliant when a wearer caught the plague

### Old idea
Until the 19th century, fossils of sea creatures found on mountains were believed to be evidence of the biblical flood.

### Turns into stone
In a kind of fossilization, the mineral opal gradually replaces the remains of animal bones and shells. It often grows in place of wood tissue, too.

# Plenty of plants

ALL OUR MOST VITAL foods come from plants. But did you know that trees and flowers also give us the deadliest poisons and life-saving medicines? The oldest of all life forms, plants have adapted with unique success to the changing planet. Plants can thrive in conditions no other living thing can tolerate, and find nutrition in the most surprising ways. Many species have evolved into fantastic colours and shapes to attract the insects and birds which carry pollen between individual specimens.

**Strong rose**
In parts of the USA, wild roses are grown in place of motorway crash barriers. As strong as metal, the bushes also prevent the cars from bouncing back into the traffic.

**Slippery slope**
Death by drowning awaits visitors to a pitcher plant. Insects are lured by sweet-smelling nectar, lose their footing on the plant's slippery sides, and fall into the lethal cocktail of rainwater and digestive acids that awaits below.

**Crying for a drink**
Plants are not silent. As they suck in moisture, they make a sound pitched too high for humans to hear.

**Rendered speechless**
The Dumb Cane plant is so-called because of its poisonous sap. Eating the leaves causes such swelling in the mouth that talking becomes impossible.

**Well-travelled pine**
Each microscopic pollen grain produced annually by a Scots pine has its own pair of balloon-like floats. These enable the pollen to travel thousands of miles in the wind. A pine tree in Scotland can fertilize another in Canada.

The desert plant Welwitschia has just two leaves, and these take 100 years to grow to full size

## Colour coded
Plants with red flowers are most successfully pollinated by birds, which are attracted by the colour. Insects, however, prefer other colours.

## Steaming through
In just one hour, an oak tree's leaves can give out 4,500 litres (990 gallons) of water vapour.

## Giant raft
Every year, the giant Amazon water lily grows up to 50 new leaves, each 183 cm (6 ft) across and strong enough to support the weight of a child.

Lupins have been grown from seed buried in the Arctic 10,000 years ago

## Prehistoric plant
In 1993, the first blooms opened on a magnolia tree grown by Japanese archaeologists from ancient seeds – the flowers were those of a species believed extinct for 1,000 years.

The foxglove is the source of the heart drug *digitalis*, a life-saving medicine

## Eye opener
*Belladonna* (Fair Lady), is another name for the Deadly Nightshade, and originates from the days when fashionable women took small doses of the plant's poison, atropine. It dilated the pupils of their eyes, making them appear larger.

## Calculating killer
Venus flytraps can count. If the hairs on its inner surface are touched just once, perhaps by a falling leaf, the plant's jaw-like lobes remain open. It takes a second touch, confirming that a victim has landed, to trigger the electrical charge that snaps the trap closed.

# Ace animals

**Hanging around**
A sloth leaves the trees only once a week – to visit its special lavatory. Sloths sleep for about 18 hours a day and move at just 4 m (13 ft) per minute.

THE ANIMAL KINGDOM abounds with countless weird and wonderful creatures with an array of diverse achievements and habits. These include unlikely athletes such as the half-tonne polar bear, which can outrun a reindeer, and the stress-management talents of the laid-back Latin American sloths, which may spend up to 20 hours of every day asleep. There are creatures, too, whose extraordinary talents have been exploited by humans – for everything from catching crooks to navigating deserts.

**White out**
To complete their camouflage, polar bears cover their black noses with a paw as they stalk prey in the snow.

A bloodhounds' sense of smell can stand as evidence in US courts

**Dogged determination**
A bloodhound can follow a trail that is over two weeks old.

**Dry rodent**
Rats can survive longer without water than camels.

While at university, the poet Lord Byron kept a pet bear in his room

**Bear trap**
Grizzly Bears sometimes roll around playfully near cattle herds. It is thought they do this to lure curious cows closer before killing and eating them.

**Walking on water**
Although basilisk lizards are 1 m (3 ft) long, they are so fleet of foot that they can run across rivers. Fringed toes barely break the surface tension, while the tail acts as a rudder.

### Behind you!
Chameleons can swivel their eyes to look in two directions at once.

### Tongue-tied
A chameleon's tongue is often twice as long as its body.

In Spain, caged chameleons are sometimes kept as fly-catchers

### Not-so-hairy ape
Baldness afflicts some monkeys in just the same way as it affects their human counterparts.

### Sandglasses
Camels can see where they are going with their eyes closed – even during fierce sandstorms. Their eyelids are transparent from the inside.

### One use for dead cats
The mummies of 300,000 cats excavated from an Ancient Egyptian temple during the last century were shipped to Liverpool in England and sold as fertilizer.

### Batty idea
During World War II, the US airforce captured 30 million bats. All were to carry a tiny incendiary bomb, fly into buildings, and explode. Fortunately, the war ended before the plan went ahead.

# Brilliant birds

IT'S A HECTIC LIFE on the wing. Birds must constantly seek food, both for the energy needed to fly, and to feed their broods of young. The workload can be astonishing. Common garden birds such as blue tits will each feed their young up to 1,500 meals a day – or 6.5 million insects in a year. Other miracles of the bird world include their nests, from the miniature perfection of a hummingbird's nest made from moss, twigs, and spiders' webs, to the eyrie once built by a North American osprey – using three shirts, a bath towel, an arrow, and a garden rake!

### An eye for an eye
The world's smallest bird, the bee hummingbird, is the same size as the eye of the world's largest bird, the ostrich.

### Long-distance lovers
The two years of Layan Albatrosses' courtship consist of solemn, waddling dances, formal bows, and crossed beaks, all with strange cries.

### Swallow that!
Migrating swallows regularly take a short cut through the 6.5-km (4-mile) long Great St Bernard road tunnel that joins Italy and Switzerland.

### Tall order
Storks have impressive appetites. One hungry bird was seen to make a meal of 44 mice, two hamsters and a frog – all in one hour.

A bird's feathers often weigh more than its entire skeleton

### Glass eggs
Penguins will ignore any egg that rolls away from the nest, but will happily sit on jam jars, cameras, or even human fists.

### You've been adopted
Newborn chicks assume the first moving object they see is their mother. Human visitors to a nest may be followed away from it by a trail of chirping chicks.

### Sense of smell
Kiwis have no tail, but they do have a nose. The long bill is tipped with nostrils for sniffing out earthworms.

### Hammer action
Woodpeckers knock on wood in search of grubs at the rate of 15 times per second. The bird's head moves at 2,000 km/h (1,300 mph) – more than twice the speed of a bullet.

Turkeys often drown in rainstorms by looking up at the sky

### Bird brain
Turkeys are so stupid that in sub-zero temperatures they can simply stand and freeze to death, even though their hutches are just a few paces away.

Flamingos' rosy colour derives from pink pigments in their diet, and fades when food is in short supply

### Beak feast
Strong swallowing muscles enable flamingos to gulp down food in their huge, sieve-like bills without raising their heads.

### High on the hog
Mouse-hunting crows have been known to sneak up unseen on their prey by riding on a pig's back.

# Under the seas

MANY SURPRISES lurk under the sea. Among its wide-open spaces, towering mountains, and black abysses dwells a fantastic diversity of creatures. Here live the largest of all animals – blue whales – and the strangest. Monsters lurk at depths where the only light is that produced by their own bodies. Giant squids and electricity-generating fish really do exist; so too do man-eating sharks that kill far fewer people than the innocent-looking puffer fish, one of the world's most poisonous creatures, and a great delicacy in Japan.

**Not so soft**
A sponge can regrow any part of its body that is eaten or torn off.

**White with anger**
Goldfish can adjust their colour according to their surroundings – they will turn pale in a white container, and dark in a black container. They also become pale when frightened or angry.

*Sharks have to keep swimming, or they will drown*

**Prawn cracker**
Pistol shrimps stun prey with shock waves from their snapping pincers.

**Scaling heights**
The climbing perch is so-called because it can leave the water and shin up trees in pursuit of insects.

*A giant squid's eyes are bigger than a human head*

**The real thing**
Giant squids don't exist only in monster movies. The North Atlantic is patrolled by fish up to 17 m (58 ft) long and two tonnes in weight.

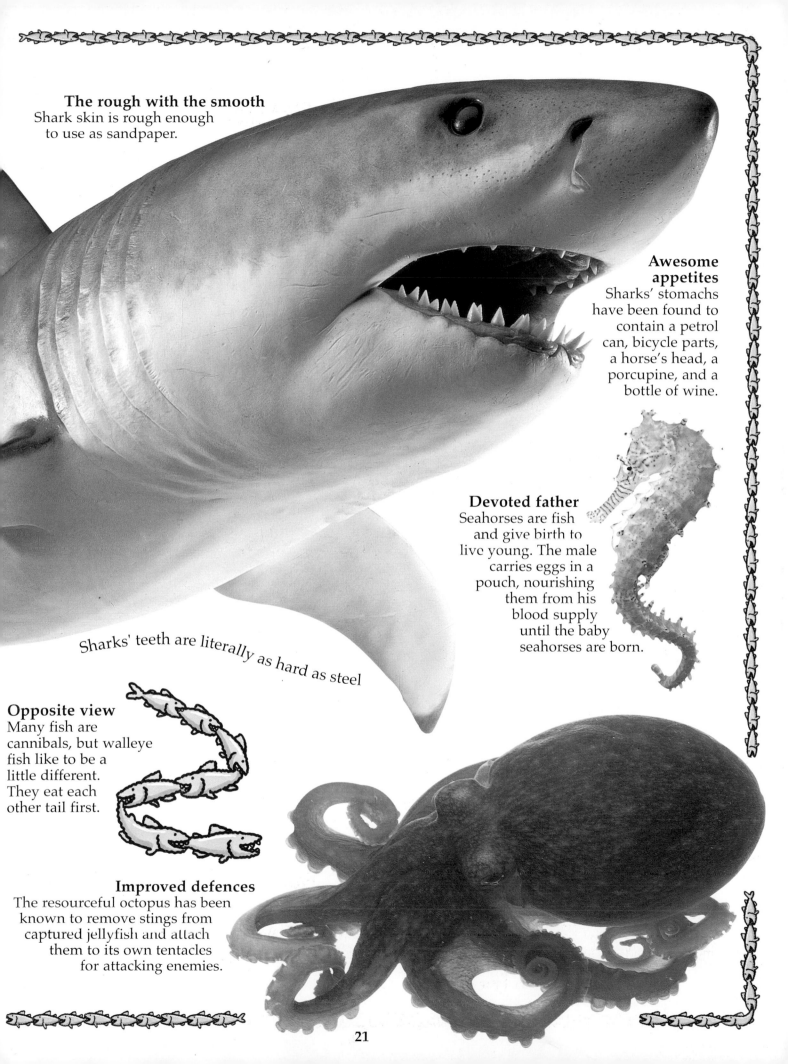

**The rough with the smooth**
Shark skin is rough enough
to use as sandpaper.

**Awesome
appetites**
Sharks' stomachs
have been found to
contain a petrol
can, bicycle parts,
a horse's head, a
porcupine, and a
bottle of wine.

**Devoted father**
Seahorses are fish
and give birth to
live young. The male
carries eggs in a
pouch, nourishing
them from his
blood supply
until the baby
seahorses are born.

Sharks' teeth are literally as hard as steel

**Opposite view**
Many fish are
cannibals, but walleye
fish like to be a
little different.
They eat each
other tail first.

**Improved defences**
The resourceful octopus has been
known to remove stings from
captured jellyfish and attach
them to its own tentacles
for attacking enemies.

# Creepy-crawlies

LOVE THEM OR LOATHE THEM, creepy-crawlies are the most successful creatures in the natural world. They are everywhere in astonishing numbers – as many in one large field as there are people in the entire world. Some of these creatures are our enemies, competing with us for food, causing illness and injury; but we have never succeeded in eliminating a single "pest" species. This is largely because many of these creatures evolve so rapidly, adapting to changes in climate, in food supply, even in colour and shape to blend with the changing environment. They were here a long time before us, and will no doubt remain long after we have gone.

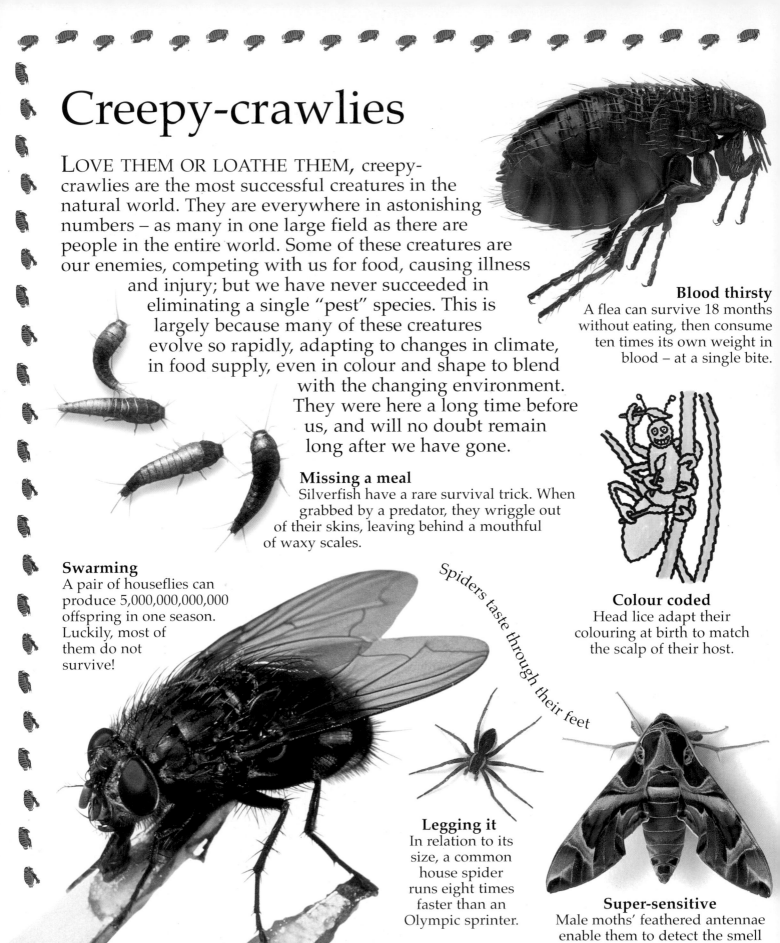

**Blood thirsty**
A flea can survive 18 months without eating, then consume ten times its own weight in blood – at a single bite.

**Missing a meal**
Silverfish have a rare survival trick. When grabbed by a predator, they wriggle out of their skins, leaving behind a mouthful of waxy scales.

**Swarming**
A pair of houseflies can produce 5,000,000,000,000 offspring in one season. Luckily, most of them do not survive!

*Spiders taste through their feet*

**Colour coded**
Head lice adapt their colouring at birth to match the scalp of their host.

**Legging it**
In relation to its size, a common house spider runs eight times faster than an Olympic sprinter.

**Super-sensitive**
Male moths' feathered antennae enable them to detect the smell of an individual female of their own species up to 10 km (6 miles) away.

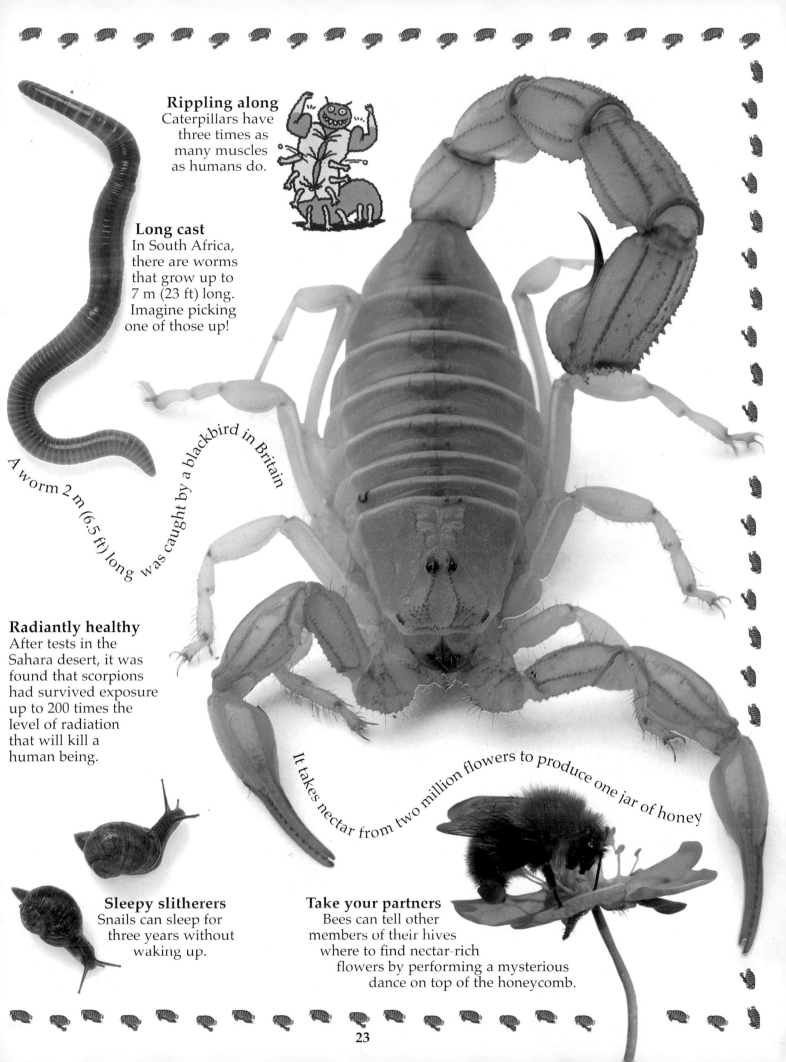

**Rippling along**
Caterpillars have three times as many muscles as humans do.

**Long cast**
In South Africa, there are worms that grow up to 7 m (23 ft) long. Imagine picking one of those up!

A worm 2 m (6.5 ft) long was caught by a blackbird in Britain

**Radiantly healthy**
After tests in the Sahara desert, it was found that scorpions had survived exposure up to 200 times the level of radiation that will kill a human being.

It takes nectar from two million flowers to produce one jar of honey

**Sleepy slitherers**
Snails can sleep for three years without waking up.

**Take your partners**
Bees can tell other members of their hives where to find nectar-rich flowers by performing a mysterious dance on top of the honeycomb.

# Resilient reptiles

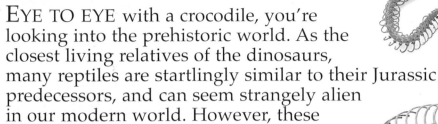

EYE TO EYE with a crocodile, you're looking into the prehistoric world. As the closest living relatives of the dinosaurs, many reptiles are startlingly similar to their Jurassic predecessors, and can seem strangely alien in our modern world. However, these sinister-looking reptiles are devoted parents. A python will gather her 100 or so eggs together and incubate them without moving for eight weeks or more. Appearances can be deceptive!

## Single mother
Unlikely though it may seem, it is in fact possible for females of some species of lizard to reproduce without mating.

## Lethal dose
Venom from a cobra is so potent that one tablespoon of the dried poison could kill over 150 people.

## Snaps them up
A hungry alligator snapping turtle wiggles the worm-like appendage on the end of its tongue – and snaps up any passing prey tempted to grab the bait.

## Seriously slim
The rare thread snake of the West Indies is *very* thin. If you removed the lead from a pencil, the snake would be able to slither through the hole.

## Heads or tails?
The shingleback lizard seems to have two heads. Its fat, waving tail fools birds into attacking the wrong end, allowing the lizard to flee.

Many snakes can delay egg fertilization for months after they have mated

## Large size
Some snakes will eat eggs that are at least twice the width of their body.

Pythons are able to fast for over a year at a time

### Swallow this
A python can devour a goat whole. After crushing the body into a sausage shape, the snake opens its jaws so wide they dislocate. The entire goat then gradually disappears into the python's cavernous mouth.

Crocodiles have only about 50 meals a year

### A smiling crocodile
While resting, crocodiles often keep their mouths open to cool off. This allows birds such as plovers to pick leftover food from between their teeth.

### Changing spectacles
Snakes have no eyelids, but the scales over their eyes are see-through. Every times a snake sheds its skin, it gets new glasses, too.

# The human body

THERE IS NOTHING more complicated than the human body. Since ancient times, scientists, philosophers, and physicians have searched for an understanding of how the body works. Their discoveries have been remarkable and fascinating, although much still remains a mystery. For example, did you know that the human body contains enough fat to produce seven bars of soap? Or that when you blush, your stomach-lining also becomes redder?

Most astronauts grow about 5 cm (2 in) during their time in space

**Touch and blow**
The next time you shake someone's hand, remember that you often carry cold viruses in the palm of your hand.

**Baby boomer**
A Russian woman in the 1700s gave birth to 69 children; 16 sets of twins, 7 sets of triplets, and 4 sets of quadruplets.

**The high life**
On average, people grow by about 8 mm (0.3 in) every night while asleep, but shrink to their usual height the following day. Pressure on the cartilage discs in the spine is relieved at night, allowing the discs to swell.

**Raise an eyebrow**
In the 18th century, fashionable people wore false eyebrows made out of mouse skin.

**You're licked!**
It is well known that every human has a unique set of fingerprints. However, did you know that everyone's tongue print is different?

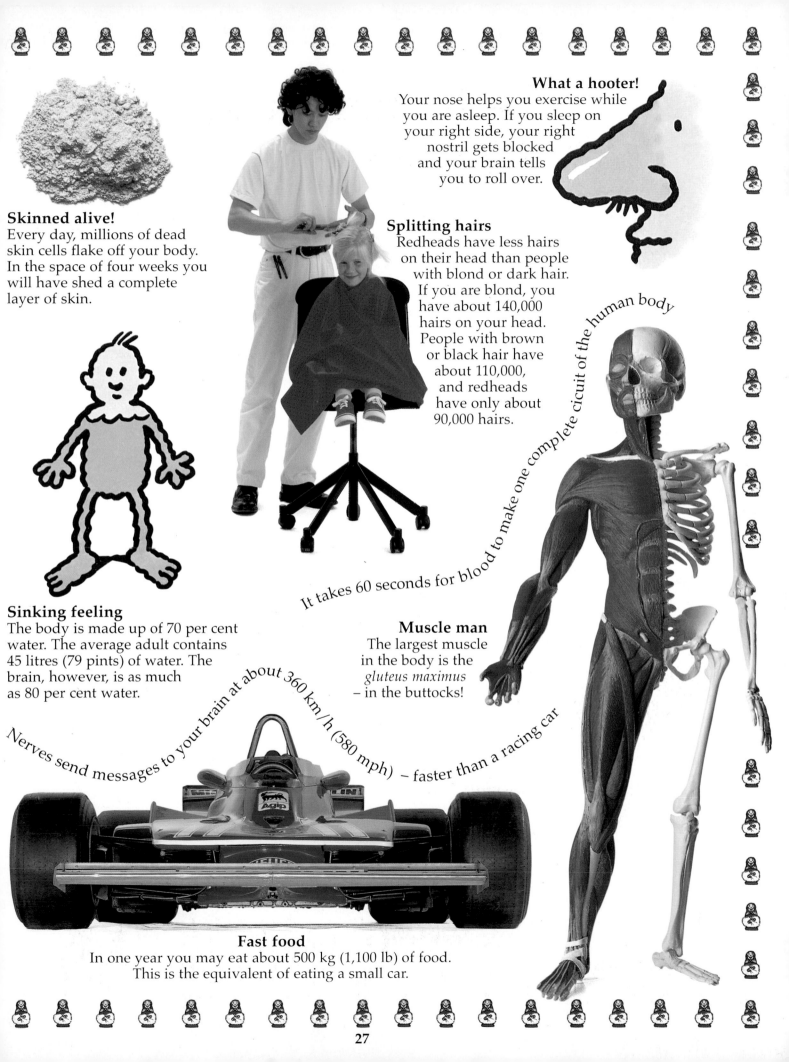

## Skinned alive!
Every day, millions of dead skin cells flake off your body. In the space of four weeks you will have shed a complete layer of skin.

## What a hooter!
Your nose helps you exercise while you are asleep. If you sleep on your right side, your right nostril gets blocked and your brain tells you to roll over.

## Splitting hairs
Redheads have less hairs on their head than people with blond or dark hair. If you are blond, you have about 140,000 hairs on your head. People with brown or black hair have about 110,000, and redheads have only about 90,000 hairs.

It takes 60 seconds for blood to make one complete cicuit of the human body

## Sinking feeling
The body is made up of 70 per cent water. The average adult contains 45 litres (79 pints) of water. The brain, however, is as much as 80 per cent water.

## Muscle man
The largest muscle in the body is the *gluteus maximus* – in the buttocks!

Nerves send messages to your brain at about 360 km/h (580 mph) – faster than a racing car

## Fast food
In one year you may eat about 500 kg (1,100 lb) of food. This is the equivalent of eating a small car.

# Food, wonderful food

THERE'S A LOT more to food than hamburgers and chips. We eat just about anything that lives – from chocolate-covered ants to dandelions – and a worldwide industry has flourished by turning the unlikeliest ingredients into processed foods for human or animal consumption. You might be surprised to know, for example, that cattle are commonly fed with fish, that seaweed is used to make ice cream, and that bird saliva is a vital ingredient in Bird's Nest soup. Delicious!

**Going short**
When food is unavailable, the ribbon worm can eat up to 95 per cent of its own body, and still survive.

**Fruit feast**
A record-breaking watermelon grown in Tennessee, USA, weighed 118 kg (260 lbs). That's enough to provide generous slices for more than 500 people.

**Sweet medicine**
Sugar and honey can be used to combat infection in emergency operations if antibiotics are not available.

In the developed world we eat an average of 64,000 kg (140,000 lbs) of food in our lifetime

**Speared**
Asparagus can be used to catch fish! During World War II, US airmen living on emergency rations of canned asparagus found that urinating into the sea drew shoals of fish – attracted by strong natural chemicals called mercaptans.

**Small cup**
It takes the harvest of an entire 2-m (13-ft) high coffee bush to produce just 450g (1lb) of beans.

**Not *that* good for you**
In 1870, a scientist reported that spinach contained ten times more iron than other vegetables. Years later it was discovered that he was wrong; in compiling his tables, he had put the decimal point in the wrong place.

### Balanced diet
Tightrope walker Charles Blondin cooked and ate an omelette while balancing over Niagara Falls, Canada.

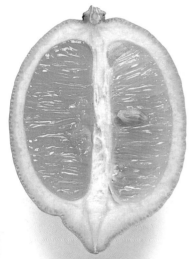

### Surprise ingredient
By weight, lemons contain more sugar than strawberries.

### Big banger
In Birmingham, England, a butcher once made a sausage that was 9 km (5.5 miles) long. This is equivalent to 87,000 sausages of a standard size.

Some soft drinks are made sweeter by adding coal

Fried mice were once used to cure smallpox in Britain

### Shell shock
Peanuts are used in the manufacture of dynamite (right), while rice forms an important ingredient in some types of cement.

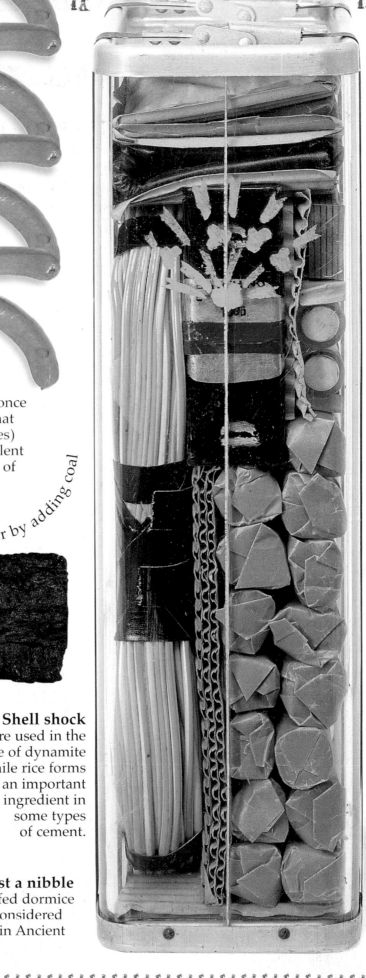

### Just a nibble
Stuffed dormice were considered a delicacy in Ancient Roman times.

# Crazy couture

THERE HAS BEEN NO EXTREME to which people haven't gone in order to be fashionable. Make-up for both sexes dates back at least 5,000 years, and if modern crazes such as nose-rings seem odd to some, consider the extraordinary fads followed by our fashionable ancestors: fantastic crinolines, multi-storey wigs, and bizarre accessories. Current *haute couture* would surely seem conservative on the same catwalk! Fashion, it seems, has always been crazy.

**Squeeze!**
To follow the fashion for an "hour-glass" figure, women in the 19th century wore corsets so tight that some suffered broken ribs and internal injuries.

**Dark side**
Suntans have not always been fashionable. For centuries, people kept their complexions pale by applying poisonous white lead.

Elizabeth I of Russia had a wardrobe of 15,000 dresses

**Beauty was only make-up deep**
Washing in the 18th century was considered unhealthy, and thick powder hid layers of dirt and facial spots. Wigs were usually made of horse hair – which didn't uncurl when it rained.

### Dressed to kill

The peplos, a tunic worn in Ancient Greece, was held together with long pins. The tunic was replaced with a new style when the pins were found to make lethal weapons.

### Sign of idleness

To show they did no manual work, wealthy people in imperial China grew their little-finger nails very long. Elaborate thimble-like covers protected the nails.

### Shades

Sunglasses were first worn by Hollywood film stars not to look "cool", but to protect their eyes against the harsh studio lights.

### Dog collar

Henry III of France often hung a basket of small dogs from his neck.

### On reflection

Elizabeth I was the first English queen to see herself in a mirror. As she grew older and her reflection became less pleasing, she banned mirrors from court.

### Combustible coiffure

Ladies' hairstyles and wigs were piled so high in the late 1700s that they ran a real risk of being set alight by chandelier candles.

A single crinoline dress could use up 1 km (1,100 yds) of lace and tulle

In the 14th century shoes reached an amazing length of 46 cm (18 in)

### Uplifting

Platform shoes have been in fashion for over 500 years. "Chopines", which could be 76 cm (30 in) high, were worn over shoes in wet weather in Renaissance Italy.

# Medicine's miracles

FIGHTING DISEASE is one of mankind's toughest challenges. Drugs and skilled surgery have triumphed over numerous illnesses, but treatments and cures for many, from cancer to the common cold, still lie in the future. As we await developments, consider the miracles of medical science – from the extraordinary but effective remedies of the ancient world, to the astounding and accidental discovery that deadly bacteria, which once killed millions, can be controlled by something as simple as mould.

*Roman barbers dressed customers' cuts with spiders' webs soaked in vinegar*

### Acid stomach?
There is enough hydrochloric acid in your digestive system to dissolve a steel nail.

### Early starter
A caesarean section, in which a baby is delivered through a cut in the mother's abdomen, is believed to be named after Roman emperor, Julius Caesar, born this way on July 12, 102 BC.

*Surgeons in Ancient Babylon were penalized if they accidentally killed a patient. Their hands were cut off!*

### Hard graft
In 1984, a boy with burns covering 98 per cent of his body was saved – with his own skin. A graft was grown from his body's own cells in a special fluid.

### Growth industry
Given enough food and warmth a bacterium could produce nearly 5,000 billion billion offspring – in just 24 hours.

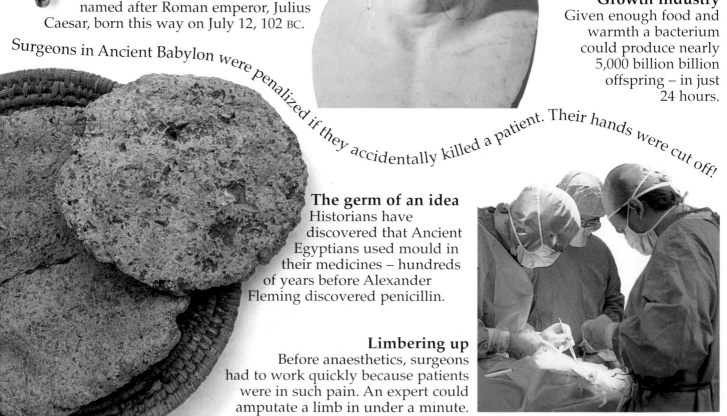

### The germ of an idea
Historians have discovered that Ancient Egyptians used mould in their medicines – hundreds of years before Alexander Fleming discovered penicillin.

### Limbering up
Before anaesthetics, surgeons had to work quickly because patients were in such pain. An expert could amputate a limb in under a minute.

## Latin blood
The Incas of South America were carrying out blood transfusions some 500 years before the technique was first successfully used in Europe in 1818.

In a lifetime, bonemarrow produces about half a tonne of blood corpuscles

## It grows back
Even if 80 per cent of your liver is removed, it can still function, and will eventually restore itself to its original size.

## Pointing the way
It is said that acupuncture was discovered when a Chinese soldier was wounded by an arrow – he found that a pain that had been troubling him for years stopped.

## Little killers
Deadly bacteria can be 1,000 times smaller than the human cells they attack. As many as 400,000 bacteria could fit on a pinhead.

# Inspired inventions

**Premier picture**
Near-blind
French inventor
Nicéphore
Niepce took the
world's first
photograph in
1826. It was
exposed for
eight hours.

IMAGINE LIFE WITHOUT air travel, or paper – or baked beans!
All owe their existence to inventors whose ingenuity accounts for
everything from the wheel to the latest soft-drink flavour. Every
invention has a story behind it. Did you know, for instance, that the
first aircraft design was on the drawing board for more than 400
years before a flight actually got off the ground? Or that the
lawnmower started life as a cloth-finishing machine?

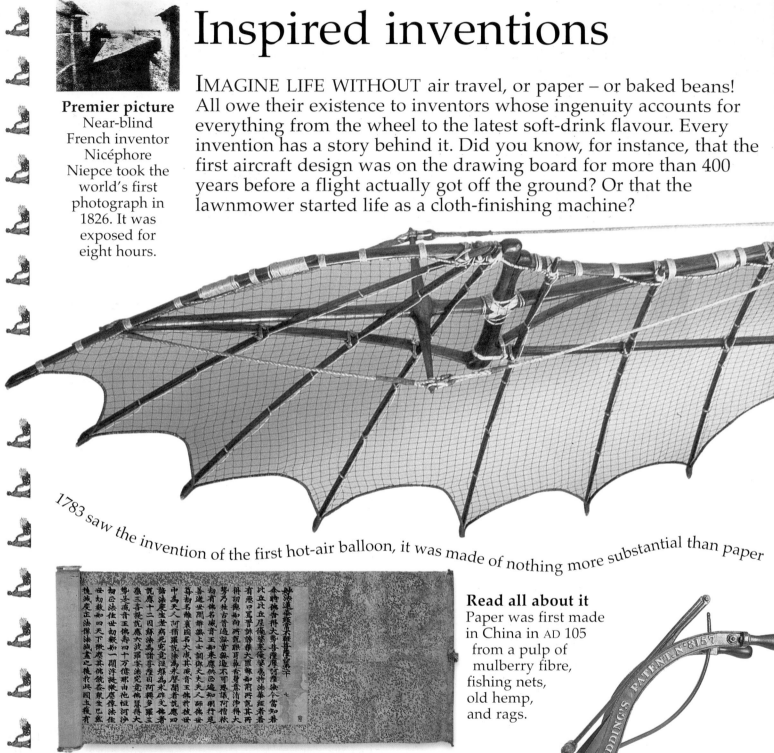

*1783 saw the invention of the first hot-air balloon, it was made of nothing more substantial than paper*

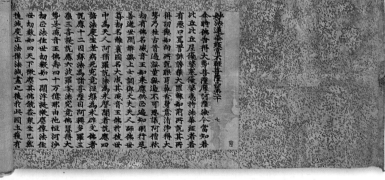

**Read all about it**
Paper was first made
in China in AD 105
from a pulp of
mulberry fibre,
fishing nets,
old hemp,
and rags.

**Late opening**
Canned food dates
from 1812, but the
first can opener was
not invented for
another 50 years!

**Out to grass**
The first lawnmower
was originally intended
as a machine for use
in the textile industry.
Realizing it could cost
many skilled workers
their jobs, the inventor
adapted it as an efficient
grass cutter instead.

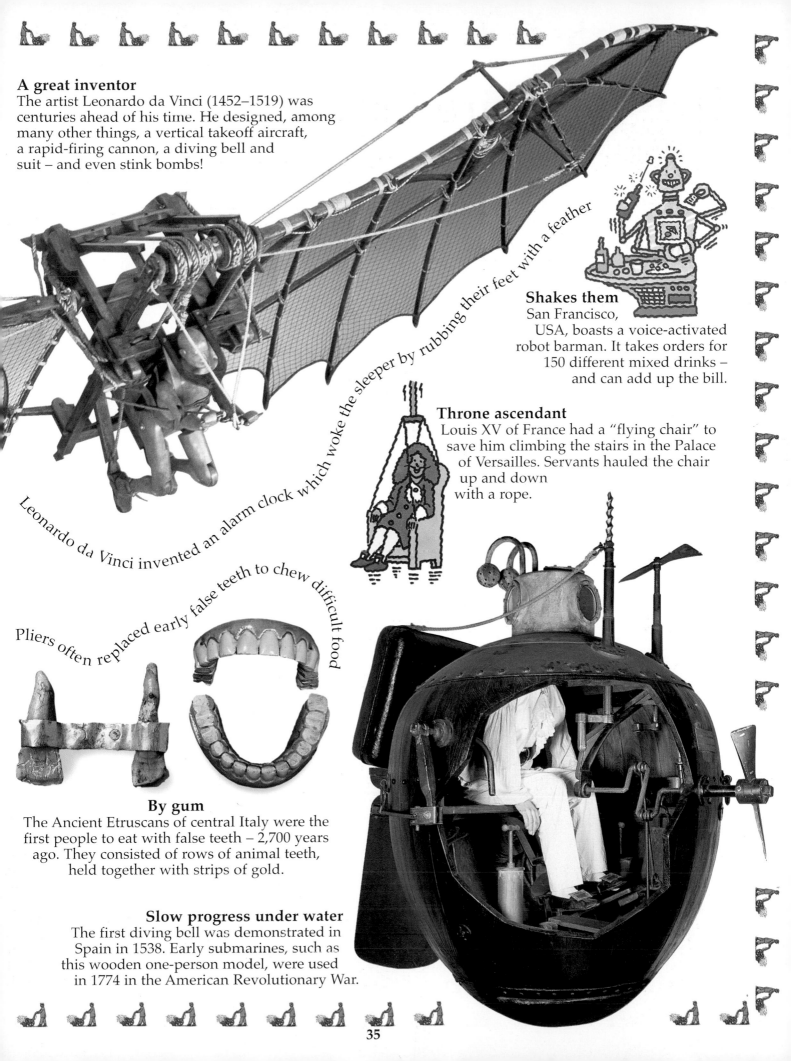

## A great inventor
The artist Leonardo da Vinci (1452–1519) was centuries ahead of his time. He designed, among many other things, a vertical takeoff aircraft, a rapid-firing cannon, a diving bell and suit – and even stink bombs!

Leonardo da Vinci invented an alarm clock which woke the sleeper by rubbing their feet with a feather

## Shakes them
San Francisco, USA, boasts a voice-activated robot barman. It takes orders for 150 different mixed drinks – and can add up the bill.

## Throne ascendant
Louis XV of France had a "flying chair" to save him climbing the stairs in the Palace of Versailles. Servants hauled the chair up and down with a rope.

Pliers often replaced early false teeth to chew difficult food

## By gum
The Ancient Etruscans of central Italy were the first people to eat with false teeth – 2,700 years ago. They consisted of rows of animal teeth, held together with strips of gold.

## Slow progress under water
The first diving bell was demonstrated in Spain in 1538. Early submarines, such as this wooden one-person model, were used in 1774 in the American Revolutionary War.

35

# Music and art

SELF-EXPRESSION dates back to prehistory. Cave paintings of animals from 20,000 years ago are the earliest evidence of our desire to communicate thoughts or ideas. Over the centuries artists and performers have been mocked, worshipped, castigated, and scorned for their surprising, awe-inspiring, or shocking works. There are no limits to what we call art. Whether it's wrapping an island in vast sheets of pink polythene, or completely filling a house with concrete, artists will always try to break the boundaries of the imagination.

## Tragic fate
Greek dramatist Aeschylus reputedly came to an unlikely end. An eagle dropped a tortoise on him, mistaking his bald head for a stone on which to break the shell.

*Seeing the beauty of the Ancient Roman paintings in Nero's palace, Raphael wrote "Raphael was here"*

## Down to Earth
The artist Raphael (1483–1520) thought the tradition of depicting angels floating in the air looked unrealistic. All of his paintings show each religious figure standing on something – even if it is only a cloud.

*The Virgin Mary is the subject of twice as many biographies as Jesus*

## Will it last?
Some contestants in America's 3,000-hour dance marathons of the 1930s used their breaks (maxium 11 minutes per hour) to get married, or even have teeth extracted.

## Changed his mind
Robert Louis Stevenson threw the first version of his story *The Strange Case of Dr Jekyll and Mr Hyde* on the fire after a quarrel with his wife, who said she hated it.

## Early music
Mozart was composing short keyboard pieces before he was six, and was only 12 when he wrote his first opera.

## Best seller
The Bible is the most widely distributed book in the world. Complete translations amount to 349 languages.

### 1 billion best tunes
The Beatles are the biggest-selling pop group in history – the only one to have sold more than a billion recordings.

### Many a slip
British author John Creasy received 743 rejection slips before his first book was published. He then went on to write nearly 600 mystery novels.

### On an unexpected note
Joseph Haydn's 96th symphony was named the "Miracle" after a chandelier crashed from the concert hall's ceiling during its first performance. No one was injured.

The shortest composition in the world is *Vexations*, lasting a minute

### Pipe dreams
The lowest notes from a large organ may come from pipes up to 10 m (32 ft) long.

STEINWAY & SONS

### Long player
The one-minute score for *Vexations* states that it should be played 840 times in succession. This lasts for 14 hours.

### Molto pianissimo
The quietest piece of music ever composed is *4' 4"* written in 1952. A pianist sits at the instrument for 4 minutes and 33 seconds, then leaves. The score is blank.

# Built to amaze

FOR THOUSANDS OF YEARS, architects and builders have been building ever-more extraordinary structures. Whether dwellings or places of work, worship, or entertainment, many of these buildings are awesome. The story of these technological achievements is an amazing one, from the 5,000-year-old Great Pyramid of Cheops in Egypt to the 20th century's soaring skyscrapers. The Channel Tunnel under the sea between England and France is an exceptional underground structure. The 50.5-km (31-mile) triple-tubed tunnel, of which 38 km (23 miles) are under the sea, took less than seven years to build.

### Leaning towers
The spires of the tallest skyscrapers can sway by up to 2 m (6 ft) in violent storms.

The colosseum was built out of the same material as today's stadiums — concrete

### Home of the gladiators
Rome's colosseum, completed in AD 80, had room for 87,000 spectators. It remained the world's largest amphitheatre until the opening of Wembley Stadium, London, in 1923.

The 4,000-year-old palace of Knossos, Crete, contains a working flush toilet

### Taking panes
Until the 19th century, glazed windows were so valuable that owners often moved them from house to house.

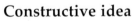

### Every convenience
In Paris, there are purpose-built public lavatories – for dogs!

### Constructive idea
Napoleon Bonaparte, who visited Egypt in 1798, calculated that the stone in the three pyramids at Giza would be sufficient to build a 4-m (13-ft) high wall around France.

The Great Pyramid is big enough to enclose the main cathedrals of Milan, Florence, Rome, and London

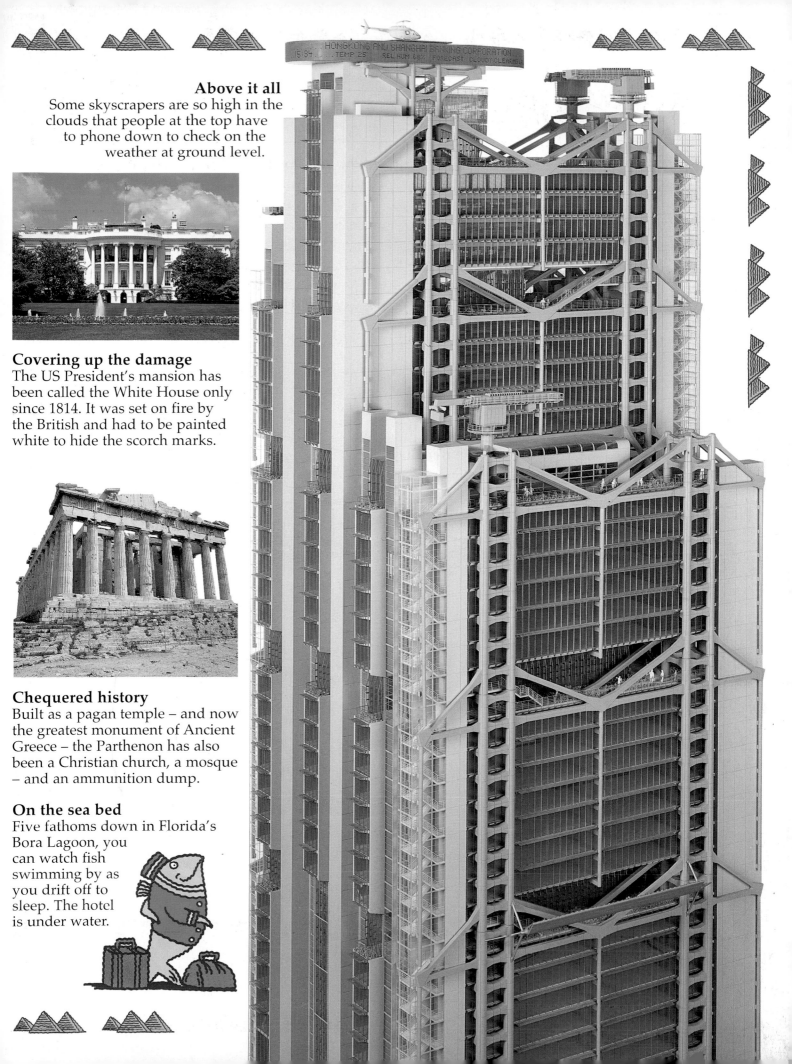

## Above it all

Some skyscrapers are so high in the clouds that people at the top have to phone down to check on the weather at ground level.

## Covering up the damage

The US President's mansion has been called the White House only since 1814. It was set on fire by the British and had to be painted white to hide the scorch marks.

## Chequered history

Built as a pagan temple – and now the greatest monument of Ancient Greece – the Parthenon has also been a Christian church, a mosque – and an ammunition dump.

## On the sea bed

Five fathoms down in Florida's Bora Lagoon, you can watch fish swimming by as you drift off to sleep. The hotel is under water.

# First class travel

THE SPEED OF TODAY'S TRANSPORT can take your breath away. You can buy a car that will exceed the speed limit by three times, or commute daily in trains that reach 300 km/h (186 mph). But the accessibility of transportation means that traffic is now so heavy that car journeys in city centres can be slower than in the days of horse-powered carriages. In the air it's a different story: aeroplanes take us to destinations on the other side of the world in a matter of hours – distances our ancestors would not have travelled in a lifetime.

### All roads stop at Rome
Reducing traffic congestion by prohibiting vehicles from cities is not a new idea. Julius Caesar tried it 2,000 years ago when he banned chariots from the centre of Rome.

In 1972, 46 students from Queensland University all crammed into a Mini

### Visionary idea
The first cars had no windscreen wipers. Drivers smeared the glass with potato or apple to help the rainwater run off.

### Kick start
The first passengers in aviation history were a cockerel, a sheep, and a duck, carried by hot-air balloon in 1783. The only injury was to the cock, which was kicked by the sheep before takeoff.

### Plenty of landing space
Saudi Arabia's King Khalid International Airport is the largest in the world at 236 sq km (91 sq miles). It is twice the size of the city of Paris, France.

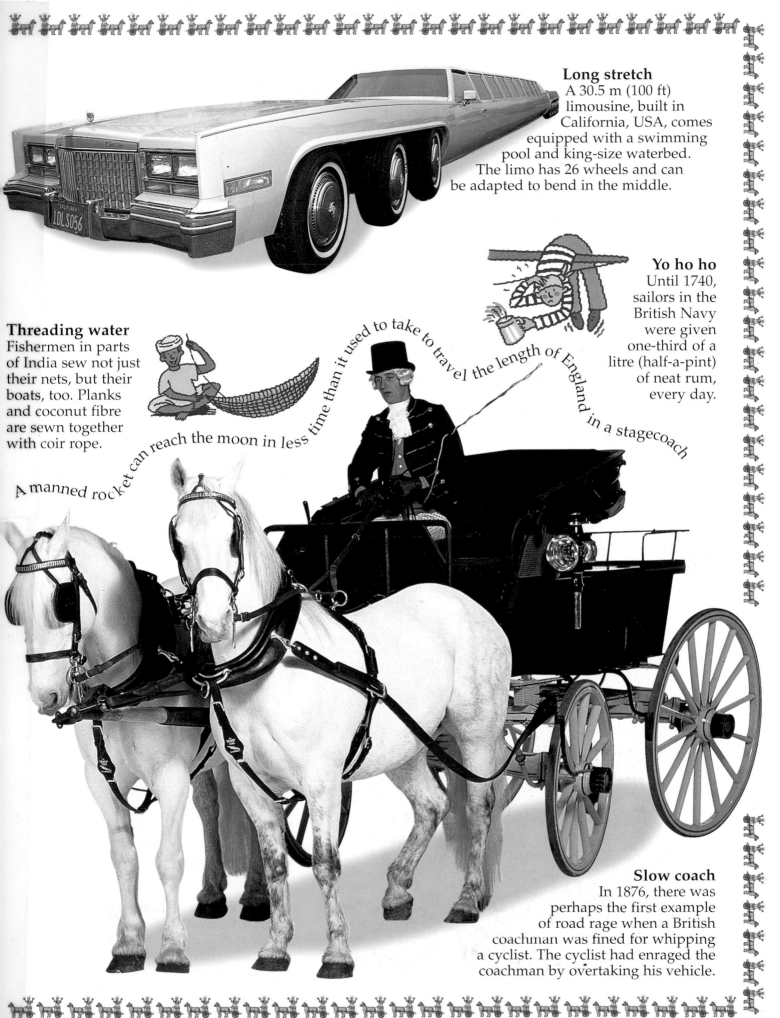

### Long stretch
A 30.5 m (100 ft) limousine, built in California, USA, comes equipped with a swimming pool and king-size waterbed. The limo has 26 wheels and can be adapted to bend in the middle.

### Yo ho ho
Until 1740, sailors in the British Navy were given one-third of a litre (half-a-pint) of neat rum, every day.

### Threading water
Fishermen in parts of India sew not just their nets, but their boats, too. Planks and coconut fibre are sewn together with coir rope.

A manned rocket can reach the moon in less time than it used to take to travel the length of England in a stagecoach

### Slow coach
In 1876, there was perhaps the first example of road rage when a British coachman was fined for whipping a cyclist. The cyclist had enraged the coachman by overtaking his vehicle.

# Spectacular sports

FROM THE FIRST-EVER 100-METRE SPRINT inside 10 seconds to the electrifying last-minute match-winning score, spectacular feats are almost everyday events in the calendar of sport. But perhaps the most astonishing aspect of sport is how seriously people take it! One football manager once summed up the game as "not a matter of life and death – it's much more serious than that." Certainly countless competitors in sports history have risked all in the pursuit of fame, and at least one war actually began on a playing field!

## It's a goal!

One of the longest scoring kicks in rugby history was a 90-m (270-ft) drop goal by Gerry Brand of South Africa against England in 1932.

*Early football games in England had teams of up to 500 players*

## Dead serious

First played in colleges and universities, American football's early days were dangerous. In the 1905 season, 18 players were killed and 150 seriously injured.

## Fine air

A baseball travels 9 per cent further in Denver, Colorado, than anywhere else in the USA. High altitude makes the air 17 per cent thinner than at sea level.

## Course record

A golfer competing in a qualifying match in Pennsylvania, USA, drove her ball into a river at the 16th hole. She reached the ball by boat, then completed the hole – in just 166 shots!

*Blind pensioner Margaret Weldon scored two holes-in-one on consecutive days*

## What an entry!

Playing a violin, Belgian musician Joseph Merlin made a sensational entrance at a masked ball in London in 1760. He was wearing the first known pair of roller skates.

## Net result

Basketball was first played in 1891, but it was another two years before anyone thought of cutting a hole in the net.

**A little luxury**
The first game of table tennis was played around 1880 – with a ball made from a champagne cork, and a pair of cigar-box lids for bats.

The game of table tennis was first called Gossamer

Golf balls were originally stuffed with feathers

**Bow under strain**
The first reference to golf in Scotland is an edict banning it in 1457. The Scots were neglecting their archery practice for golf – King James IV had no choice but to outlaw the game.

# Index

# Acknowledgements

The publisher would like to thank the following for their kind permission to reproduce photographs:

t= top, b = bottom, l = left, r = right, c = centre
AKG London: 36c; Apple Corps Ltd 37tl; Bridgeman Art Library/Giraudon: 32c; British Library: 36cb/Laurence Pordes: 34clb; British Museum/Peter Hayman 17bc, 30 tr; Jean-Loup Charmet: 34tl; Corbis-Bettman: 36tr; ET Archive/Archaeological Museum, Lima: 33tr; Robert Harding Picture Library: 39cl;

Imagebank: 37clb; NASA: 8c, tl, 9 c.; Mike Dunning, Science Museum: tr, 10bl; Oxford Scientific Films/Z. Lesczynski: 24tl; Rex Features Ltd: 39 tl, 40br, 41tl; Science Photo Library/Ross Lappa: 12crb/Ulrike: 32br/Dr Tony Brain & David Parker; Jerry Young: 33cb, 17 bl & tr, 18 cr, 22 cr & bl, 24 c & br, 25r, 41 cb; 24–25 ct Natural History Museum; Frank Spooner Pictures: 13 cl; Barleylands Farm Museum and South of England Rare Breeds Centre 40cr.

**Photographers**
Geoff Brightling, Jane Burton, Peter Chadwick, Andy Crawford, Geoff Dann, Philip Dowell,

Andreas von Einsiedel, Steve Gorton. Alan Hills, Christi Graham & Nick Nicholls (British Museum), Peter Griffiths, Bob Guthany, Dave King, Liz McAulay, Andrew McRobb, Ray Moller, Brian D. Morgan, The Moscow Museum, Royale Newport, Frank Greenaway, Colin Keates (Natural History Museum), Stephen Oliver, Roger Phillips. James Stevenson (National Maritime Museum). Karl Shone, Clive Streetor, Kim Taylor.

With many thanks also to Dorian Davies for creating the cartoons, and to Alex Clifford for design assistance.
**Jacket designer** Tony Chung.